H.E.A.R.T.

CASSIE CAMPBELL

& LORNA SCHULTZ NICHOLSON

D0870086

Fenn Publishing Company Ltd.

Bolton, Canada

Fenn Publishing Company Ltd.

H. E. A. R. T.

A Fenn Publishing Book / First Published in 2007

Fenn Publishing Company Ltd.
Bolton, Ontario, Canada
www.hbfenn.com

The publisher gratefully acknowledges the support of the Canada Council for the Arts and the Ontario Arts Council for its publishing program.

We acknowledge the support of the Government of Ontario through the Ontario Media Development Corporation's Ontario Book Initiative.

THE CANADA COUNCIL | LE CONSEIL DES ARTS
FOR THE ARTS | DU CANADA
SINCE 1957 | DEPUIS 1957

ONTARIO ARTS COUNCIL
CONSEIL DES ARTS DE L'ONTARIO

We acknowledge the financial support of the Government of Canada through the Book Publishing Industry Development Program (BPIDP) for our publishing activities.

Care has been taken to trace ownership of copyright material in this book and to secure permissions. The publishers will gladly receive any information that will enable them to rectify errors or omissions.

Design: First Image
Printed and bound in Canada

Library and Archives Canada Cataloguing in Publication

Campbell, Cassie, 1973-
    HEART / Cassie Campbell, Lorna Schultz-Nicholson.

ISBN 978-1-55168-315-7

    1. Campbell, Cassie, 1973- --Juvenile literature. 2. Women hockey players--Canada--Biography--Juvenile literature.
I. Schultz Nicholson, Lorna II. Title.

GV848.5.C36A3 2007   j796.962092   C2007-903067-X

CONTENTS

FOREWORD

Wayne Gretzky

I first met Cassie in 1998. Since then I've watched her play and lead her team as captain to secure gold medals in both the 2002 Salt Lake City and the 2006 Turin Olympics. During both of those Olympic Games, I was totally impressed with her ability to motivate the Canadian women's team both on and off the ice. Not only did she work hard as a player during the actual games but she seemed to go above and beyond her duties as captain to try to keep her team together off the ice. Cassie is the only Canadian hockey player who has captained back to back Olympic gold medals. I truly believe she has been able to take the women's game to another level by being a strong leader.

Cassie has also worked really hard to promote the women's game by being a true ambassador of the sport. To me that is important because it is a game I love so much. I know I'm lucky to have had such a great career in hockey and it is obvious that Cassie thinks she is lucky, too. I think it's important to give back to our sport and share what we've learned. I'm honoured to write this foreword for Cassie because I know she truly loves our great game and wants to tell you about her great experiences.

I know that if you read this book you'll become a better hockey player, but more importantly you will become a better person as this book has great tips on hockey and on life.

FOREWORD

I have known Cassie for well over ten years – having spent a significant part of my hockey career playing along her side on the national women's team. I have witnessed her in many roles, including: as a player; a teammate; team captain; and, as a close friend. I was truly honoured when she asked me to write the foreword to her book.

As a player, Cassie was great both offensively and defensively. Some players have specific strengths but Cassie could do it all. She is one of a select few to have played forward and defence at the international level while excelling at both positions. I believe her work ethic is what made her so dominant. She worked hard on every aspect of her game, both on and off the ice. She would often stay late after practice to work on something she felt needed improvement as Cass was never satisfied with just average.

She was a very humble player and never gave herself enough credit. She was a pesky forechecker, a gifted playmaker, reliable defensively and although she may not agree, a talented goal scorer. Most hockey players, even the successful ones, have one, two, or, if they're very talented, three such qualities. Through hard work, determination, and sheer force of will, Cassie possessed them all.

As a teammate and captain, Cassie taught me that being a great leader and team player is not just about individual skill but about knowing how you can best contribute to the team's success. She did whatever it took to make the team better as a whole, never putting herself first. This is what made her such a great leader and captain. She was honest, genuine and lead the team by example. She had a positive attitude – always giving 100% of herself and encouraged us even if she was having a tough day herself. Cass would be the first one to praise someone for her efforts and successes but would also be the first one to challenge a teammate if she believed she had more to give.

Training and competing for the national team is always a constant battle. It's easy to fall into the trap of thinking about yourself only and worrying about your individual performance, but Cass never did that, and she never let her teammates do that. That focus is a

Vicky Sunohara

big reason why Canada was so successful during her years on the team - particularly her years as captain.

As a friend, Cassie is one of the most caring and generous people I have ever known. She will lend a hand to anyone who needs help. One of her greatest qualities is the respect she has for every person she meets regardless of who they are or what they do. Although she has accomplished so much in her life, she remains grounded and modest. One of the things that the general public might not know about Cassie is that she has always had a great, and quirky, sense of humour. She has the amazing ability to make a stressful situation easier to deal with. Whether it be a joke, a song or a dance, Cassie is never afraid to laugh at herself or have others laugh at her. She is a lot of fun to be around and seems to have a way of drawing people to her.

Cassie has been and continues to be a great role model for many, including me. I think the most motivating words that she could hear are, "you can't do that." She will prove you wrong every time. Cassie was the face of women's hockey in Canada for a long time, and we couldn't have had a better spokesperson. Now that her playing career is over, she's still helping to develop the female game in Canada. Her broadcasting career is but one example of the doors she continues to open for women's hockey, female athletes, and women in general. In the little spare time she has, she works tirelessly for many charities, including her annual ball hockey tournament, which raises money for Ronald McDonald House.

I have had the chance to meet most of Cassie's family and it is not surprising that she has become so successful. They are great people and have been there for her through good and tough times. She is extremely proud of her nieces and nephews and loves to spend time with them whenever she can. Her best friend and husband, Brad, is her rock. I can't remember a conversation we have had that she hasn't mentioned how much he means to her and how supportive he is.

I used to think that good things only happened to people who were lucky but, with Cassie as an example, I now know that nothing comes easy. I am amazed at all that she has accomplished in such a short time and I am very excited to see what else she will do in the future. For Cassie, I know the sky is the limit!

INTRODUCTION

I thought of the idea for *H.E.A.R.T.* during the 1998 Olympic year. At that time, it was just an idea. I am so glad that I waited until my playing career was over to actually come out with a finished publication because I have learned so much since then. This book would not have been complete had I done it before now.

I played on the national team for 13 seasons, and over the years I have met some great people. Everyone I played with or worked with has had a big impact on my life and has helped to move the female game of hockey forward. I learned valuable lessons from some of the greatest captains, like Sue Scherer and France St. Louis. I've weathered so much with my teammates to push our game to new heights. Playing hockey for Team Canada was so much fun, and I will remember every moment.

When the opportunity to write a book came along, I really didn't want to write it on just myself—instead, I wanted to share stories of my teammates and friends. This book includes stories that have never been told.

I couldn't put all the stories into this one book, but I wanted to tell as many as I could. I wanted to share with you my teammates' dedication and passion to our sport. I hope my stories show you why I think so many of the people in women's hockey are amazing and genuinely love the game.

H.E.A.R.T., to me, is the essence of every Canadian hockey player, whether male or female. It is the reason why Canada is so successful in hockey. I want you to know that in order to be successful you, too, can do these simple things.

I hope you enjoy this book. I hope you get as much out of it as I did while working on the project.

I hope you live life with *H.E.A.R.T.*

Cassie Campbell

H =
HARD WORK

"Hard work builds the foundation of champions. Without it, you become complacent and mediocre."

Cassie Campbell

Success takes hard work. Sure, some people have natural skill, but that will take them only so far. No athlete or successful person can rely on just skill to excel. No matter how much talent you've been given, you have to constantly work hard to improve. I was cut from the 1990 and 1992 national teams, and it took commitment and hard work to get me to where I wanted to go.

At the 2006 Olympics in Turin, Italy, the Canadian women's hockey team won the gold medal. I think we won gold because we worked extremely hard. It almost seemed too easy when all was said and done, but I attribute our success to our fitness level and our training ethics. We took the women's game to another level, and we were determined to defend our 2002 title.

Before we landed in Italy, we had played some 50 games, more than any NHL team up to that point and more than we had ever played together as a national team. We had trained and trained for this event. All my teammates agreed that it was definitely the toughest year of on- and off-ice training, combined with a crazy travel schedule. There were many moments during the year when my body wanted to quit. Had I listened to the voice in my head, I wouldn't have my second Olympic gold medal today. I'm so thankful that I continued. It's important for you to know that all athletes have moments where they have bad days and think about quitting. No matter what activity or sport you choose, if you want to be successful, you must persevere, and this means you have to work hard and prepare. Working hard and pushing through even your bad days is the key to success.

> *We took the women's game to another level, and we were determined to defend our 2002 title.*

In June 2005, nine months before the 2006 Olympics, the Canadian national women's hockey team held its training camp in Prince Edward Island. Normally, I don't mind training camps, but, wow, was I was in for a shock! This was the most intense camp that I had ever attended. Some mornings when the alarm went off, I would lay there and think, "I don't want to get up." We would have all crawled into bed at 11:00 p.m. or later the night before after an evening of some sort of activity, only to get up at 6:30 a.m. the next morning.

> *At that point in my career, I knew hard work would take me a long way, and I knew that as a team, we had to prepare.*

I would drag myself out of bed anyway. Why? Because all my teammates felt the same as me, and I could not disappoint them. I wanted to win gold again. I wanted another Olympic medal around my neck. I wanted to make the team. I knew I was a veteran, and I knew there were lots of young girls trying out who were solid hockey players. At that point in my career, I knew hard work would take me a long way, and I knew that as a team, we had to *prepare*.

Sometimes, we worked out five times or more a day. For one of the weeks, we crossed Prince Edward Island on our bikes every morning, riding over 100 kilometres a day. I like mountain biking, but I am not really a biker; therefore, I had to push myself a little harder. The camp was about team-building and perseverance, and it was run in a creative manner to maximize ultimate fitness. No matter what, every day, we rode as hard as possible to get across that line. After the biking was over, it was on to lifting weights and enduring an abdomen workout, followed by a game of soccer or floor hockey or a run or a swim. It was the hardest training I'd ever done. It was the hardest training any of us had ever done. It was three weeks of gruelling boot camp.

By February 2006, when it was time to fly to Italy, each of us was in top shape. We arrived in Italy a week early so that we could get used to the time change, and were taken to the small village of Torre Pellice. This was to be our last block of training time before the Games began. Even after our extensive preparation, practice games, and workouts, we still had to do

Charlottetown, PEI, at the end of our long four-day bike trip. There is just one more day of a three-week camp to go – the triathlon.

Hayley Wickenheiser, me, and Vicky Sunohara with our gold medals from Turin in 2006.

bike sprints and physical training. Collectively we thought, "Honestly, can we not have a break prior to starting the Games? Why are we continuing with all of this training?" We were told that hard work was necessary to maintain our fitness level for game time. Even during the last week before the Olympics, when one would think that we had perfected our game, we were training as hard as ever, attempting to improve even more.

Playing at the national level has allowed me the privilege of working with incredibly talented women. My teammate Cheryl Pounder is someone who, through fitness concentration alone, took her game to the next level. She never took a moment off and always gave 100 percent. She made the team in 1994—at the young age of 18—and then was cut and didn't return until 1999. Through those in-between years, she never stopped training. Cheryl was the sort of player we all wanted on our team because we knew she'd never give up. She worked her way up through sheer determination and hard work to provide that big defence for our 2002 and 2006 Olympic teams.

We were told that hard work was necessary to maintain our fitness level for game time.

Hayley Wickenheiser is another player recognized for her hard work and preparedness. Even with the success she enjoyed during and after 2002, she continued to train harder and harder. To me, she's someone who could have easily taken her talent for granted and eased up, but she didn't. Hayley is one of the best female hockey players in the world, and she's never satisfied with yesterday. She continually works in a shooting gallery and trains in a gym to improve. Hayley is such a consistent player because she works to her full potential in every moment of her on- and off-ice training program. What people see on the ice is the excellence she practices every single day. Cheryl and Hayley, and anyone who has ever been in the program, know what it means to work hard to take the women's game to the next level.

It was plain and simple hard work that got us the gold medal in Turin in 2006. When it was draped around my neck, I couldn't stop staring at it. As I looked at my teammates, I saw such expressions of joy on each of their faces. I stood on the blueline beside Hayley Wickenheiser and Vicky Sunohara with tremendous pride, having defended our gold medal from 2002. I knew all the hard work was worth it because it allowed me to feel this amazing moment for a second time. To be successful, you must work hard and prepare. And I know from our 2006 performance that success is worth so much more when you have gone above and beyond to get there!

> *It was plain and simple hard work that got us the gold medal in Turin in 2006.*

Hockey has taught me many valuable lessons, one of which is the need to incorporate creativity with hard work, especially when battling back from an injury. During the last game of our 2004 season in the National Women's Hockey League (NWHL) finals, I took a hit while in an awkward position. I kept playing, not thinking too much of it. The next day, however, I went for an MRI and learned that I had suffered a concussion and had a bruised spinal cord in my neck. I had to see a neurologist and a neurosurgeon. Both doctors told me to rest and take some time off because I had a serious concussion and a neck too weak to hold my head. As an athlete, it's hard to take time off. There is the fear of falling behind and losing ground to the many healthy and fit athletes who are anxious to take your spot.

I could have quit playing hockey at this time. And believe me, the thought crossed my mind. The diagnosis given to me by my doctor was scary, and I had to think of not just my health as a hockey player but also my health for the rest of my life.

Vicky and I on an eight-hour plane ride to Turin and a seven-hour time difference, a big adjustment to make in a short time.

I already had a gold medal from Salt Lake City and a silver medal from Nagano. But I loved the game, and that kept me motivated.

So I didn't quit.

> *Here I had spent my entire summer in rehab therapy, and nothing I had done had worked.*

I rehabilitated all summer long, and in the fall I stepped back on the ice. At one of the first practices, a routine hit left me in pain. I went back to the doctors and found out that I had concentrated my rehabilitation on the wrong type of neck injury. Here I had spent my entire summer in rehab therapy, and nothing I had done had worked.

Okay, so I thought of quitting again. It was a frustrating time, not knowing if I would ever be able to play again. The 2006 Olympics were still two years away, and that seemed like a long time, though something pushed me to keep going. Once I made the decision to keep playing, I knew I couldn't just sit back and relax, only going to the occasional physiotherapy session and hoping to get better. I had to do something to keep up with my teammates. What could I do?

First off, I hired a personal trainer, James Gattinger. He worked with me in Calgary to strengthen my neck and upper back so that I could physically play hockey again. He was terrific, and he introduced me to revolutionary exercises that I had never done before. While my teammates were on the ice practising and playing games, I was running hills and lifting weights. I was back to the basics, working on core exercises.

Then I hired a shooting coach to help improve my skills. Looking back, I now know this was a good move. At the time, I didn't feel that I was working as hard as everyone else, but in reality, I was. This was the way I could work, the way my health would let me work. It didn't mean I was working less,

Rower Marnie McBean, Vicky Sunohara, and I at the closing ceremonies in Turin, Italy, in February 2006.

The team during our training days in P.E.I. after playing a little friendly baseball.

just differently. Had I not been creative with my hard work, I don't think I'd have a gold medal from the 2006 Olympics in Turin, Italy. Someone would have taken my spot on the team because, most likely, my body would not have been healthy enough to play.

I remember being on the rink in Calgary all by myself, skating and doing drills that kept me in shape for my return. It wasn't always fun, but it had to be done.

I didn't step on the ice with my teammates for almost eight months. As an elite athlete, that's a long time. When I did return, just after Christmas, my first game was horrible. I knew that all eyes were on me, and as a result, I was nervous. There were only ten games remaining before Hockey Canada made the picks for the 2005 IIHF World Women's Championship team, and I had to show that I was ready to play. In the next game, I performed much better and managed to pick up three points. Then everything kicked in. I played well for the rest of the selection games and made the team with the distinguished honour to be named team captain again. In the spring of 2005, I was able to travel to Sweden for the World Championship.

> *I didn't step on the ice with my teammates for almost eight months. As an elite athlete, that's a long time.*

So, when you're limited, which happens to a lot of athletes, you have to think outside the box and create your own hard work.

And sometimes, you have to leave your comfort zone to be successful. In 1999, we were in Finland for the World Championship and our trainers decided to do a leg flush routine to get the lactic acid out of our muscles. Such a routine enhances performance and increases a player's speed the following day. First, we sat in a hot sauna. Then, when the sweat was dripping off our bodies, we had to run from the hot sauna to the freezing lake. This was in the winter! Our legs would tingle and go numb. It was crazy. I couldn't see the point of this training. But we did it anyway, and mentally, it made us tougher. So, leaving the comfort zone, mentally, is important.

It's also important sometimes to leave that comfort zone in your physical training and to challenge yourself. I'm a good runner. I like running, and it comes easy to me. Put me on a bike, and I'm not so good. I don't know why, but biking is a challenge for me. My legs burn, I struggle, and it just hurts. I love mountain biking, but training on a bike is not one of my strengths. One summer, I decided to take the hard road and bought a bike with the intention of replacing my runs with bike rides. I wanted to come out of my comfort zone to be better and fitter.

> *I'm a good runner. I like running, and it comes easy to me. Put me on a bike, and I'm not so good.*

Hard work means not taking shortcuts. In life, everyone knows and recognizes the individuals who take shortcuts. In a team setting, it is always easy to see the players who take shortcuts because they are the ones who stand out in a negative way. And everyone knows who works hard because they are your leaders. If your coach tells you to skate to the blueline or run with your soccer ball to the end of the field, do exactly what you're told to do. It's more important to do the drill properly than to win the race. And believe me, your coaches and your teammates know the athletes who make only a half stop at the blueline instead of a full stop. And the fact is that there are no shortcuts in a game. So why take shortcuts in practice? You're just defeating yourself if you cheat.

Hard work is rewarding, and it builds good work habits for anything you do in life. After the Salt Lake City 2002 Olympics, I accepted a four-month job with the NHL Network as an analyst. This job was a challenge for me, as I was an inexperienced woman in a primarily male-dominated profession. I had my

One of our intense workouts in a gym in P.E.I. leading up to the 2006 Olympics,
the most intense preparation of my career. Sometimes we worked out five times a day!

Vicky Sunohara and I hold a Canadian flag just moments after winning gold in Turin.

gold medal but little television experience, so there was a lot that I had to prove. I was scheduled to show up for work at 5:00 p.m., though I arrived no later than 3:00 p.m. every day to demonstrate my dedication. Each morning, I would begin my day with breakfast, followed by hours of research; I would read every national newspaper's sports section and scour the internet to make sure I was up-to-date on all the current happenings. At the end of my four months, I was congratulated for the excellent work I had provided. Those pats on the back were the result of hard work and preparedness. I didn't take anything for granted—neither in my professional hockey career nor my private life. There was no way I was going to just show up for this opportunity and be a token person. Yes, I was a gold medalist, but that didn't automatically make me a good television sports analyst. Again, I wanted to excel, and again, I knew the only way to excel was to work hard. I remember a producer on the show admitting to me after the season was over that when the staff found out that I got the job, they thought they would have to cover for me and that their jobs would be made much more difficult. He admitted to me that they were impressed with not only my knowledge of the game but also, more important, how hard I worked.

Remember, preparation and hard work builds the foundation of champions. Don't just do what is necessary—do what it takes, and more.

> *Yes, I was a gold medalist, but that didn't automatically make me a good television sports analyst.*

CHAPTER TWO

E = EXPERIENCE/ EDUCATION

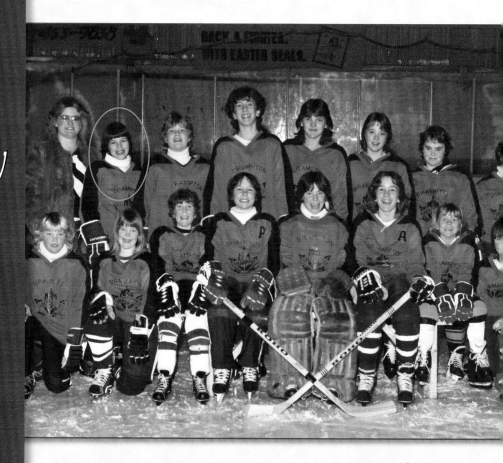

"Experience is life lessons given to you on a daily basis. You can either overlook them or pay attention to them."

Cassie Campbell

To be successful, you have to show up to your practice or classes at school with a determination to learn. By just going through the motions, you fail to see the opportunities as experiences. Everything you do is an opportunity to learn new things and meet new people. You can go to school every day to learn something. You can go to practice every day to learn something. To gain experience, however, you must realize that there is a difference between just showing up and showing up and contributing.

I remember that when I was nine years old, I desperately wanted to go to the Eddie Shack Hockey School in Ontario, near my hometown of Brampton. But it was an all-boys' hockey school, so I was nervous to go. I could have told my mother, "No, I don't want to go. I don't know anybody." I remember being scared. Instead, I went with a determination to have fun and fit in. You can step up and take risks or sit back and be complacent. I prefer to take risks.

Experience is not gained from just winning alone. Sometimes you can learn more through losing. When you lose, it is important to think about the loss, analyze why it happened, and discover what can be learned from it. This process is called *reflecting,* and I think it's an important step in improving.

> **To be successful, you have to show up to your practice or classes at school with a determination to learn.**

My first Olympic experience was in 1998. Here, my teammates and I encountered such reflection. Our women's hockey team was favoured to win the gold medal, and everyone in Canada expected us to win. We'd consistently beaten everyone in other competitions. I thought we'd worked hard, and I thought we would win.

During our round robin game against the U.S.A., we had a 4–1 lead going into the third period, though we ended up on the wrong end of a 7–4 score. It was as if we ran out of gas.

This became a big media story, and hockey fans across Canada questioned what was wrong with our team. Since we had won all previous round-robin games, we were slotted to play the U.S.A. in the gold medal game.

When we lost the final game to the U.S.A. 3–1, I was devastated. Our team never clicked in that game. We were sluggish and inconsistent. I know I didn't play my best. The year before, I had been an all-star defenceman, so perhaps I had gone into the Olympic competition complacent, thinking I was better than I was. I also got caught up in the media swirl. It was the first Olympics that recognized women's hockey, and it was the first time that I'd really been challenged in front of my country. The games we played with the U.S.A. were so close. The pressure overwhelmed us, and they got better while we didn't. After our big loss, the media decided to centre me out. Attention seemed to be on certain players, and I was one of those players. I had rested on my laurels at that Olympic tournament, which just wasn't enough to secure a gold medal. For me, I needed to play better. And I knew I needed to improve physically. I never wanted to feel that way after a loss again.

> *After our big loss, the media decided to centre me out. Attention seemed to be on certain players, and I was one of those players.*

I felt I had let my team down by not being the best I could be. For the first few months after the loss, I pointed the finger at other people. It wasn't until I woke up one day and pointed the finger at myself that I truly learned from this experience. I needed to wake up and use the loss as an experience to improve. Upon reflection, I realized my fitness level was poor. No matter what, when things go wrong, you can't blame the referees, other teammates, the media, your coaches, or your parents. You can look only at yourself to answer the question "Why?" Once you ask that question, then—and only then—will you learn from

An action shot of me during my days as captain. I wore number 77 in recognition of my childhood idol, Paul Coffey.

the experience. The 1998 Olympic loss taught me a lot about myself, and it made me a better person and player.

To learn from any experience, you must reflect and think about your strengths and weaknesses. Winning the silver medal in 1998 against a team that we had previously beaten before the final game taught me so much about my weaknesses. I learned I wanted to be healthier and stronger so that I could play better in the forthcoming 2002 Olympics in Salt Lake City. I played that tournament in peak physical condition.

> *I wanted to be healthier and stronger so that I could play better in the forthcoming 2002 Olympics in Salt Lake City.*

I reflected on what I needed to improve and then went out and worked hard to be the athlete I knew I could be. You can learn as much from losing as you can from winning. There were things I really needed to learn, and the loss forced me to do so. Had we won, maybe I wouldn't have had such a great learning opportunity. The loss made me question my own complacency but gave me the opportunity to come up with some solutions. Challenges will occur in your life, and it is how you respond to those challenges that make you stand out from the rest.

I really respect young players who enter the Hockey Canada program with open eyes and a willingness to learn. Some young players come in thinking that they deserve everything but have yet to earn anything. Sarah Vaillancourt and Gillian Apps are two young players of whom I think highly. They are both fit, work hard in practice, and are true team players. They are natural leaders because they have never expected anything. They were willing to gain experience and learn from everything and everyone around them. They took the lumps instead of saying, "I'm going to be a star right away." And yes, they were stars in their own community, so coming to our camp and being put on the bottom of the ladder must have been challenging for them as young players. I loved that they were willing to play any role—without complaint.

In life, you are going to make mistakes. The key is to learn from your mistakes. Sometimes, you may say the wrong thing after an experience. And sometimes, you need to own up and apologize. Apologizing is not a bad thing, as long as you don't continue to make the same mistake and keep saying sorry. From a team point of view, it's important to forgive and apologize. I have been guilty of doing and saying the wrong things at the wrong times. It happens, and, in the heat of the battle, it sometimes happens very quickly.

Apologizing is not a bad thing, as long as you don't continue to make the same mistake and keep saying sorry.

We all make mistakes, but learning how to deal with them is what is important.

Experience happens everywhere, every day, and is not contained just to the ice, field, or court. After winning gold in 2002, I was asked by the Hospital for Sick Children in Toronto to be part of a PSA (public service announcement) to be filmed with a young girl. I felt extremely stressed when returning home from the Olympics. I was busy but wanted to use my success in a way that could offer some good. I remember arriving at the hospital and being introduced to the young girl who was battling cancer. I was supposed to be there for only an hour, but the PSA took longer than planned, and I was there for three hours. During my visit, the little girl required her scheduled needles. I asked if I should leave, though the nurses indicated that it would be fine for me to stay.

When the needle entered her arm, she briefly cried and then looked at me and apologized for crying. At that moment, I realized my stress paled in comparison to hers. She was an incredibly strong individual, and by the end of the experience, I felt as if we had created a bond. We exchanged contact information, and when her mother called me two days later, I thought she was phoning to thank me for my time. But sadly, she was calling to tell me that her daughter had passed away. This experience taught me many things—most important, that I was lucky that I still had my life. It gave me great perspective. I will never forget the little girl who showed so much courage as she battled cancer.

As a young person involved in sports and activities, you might get caught up in stressful decisions such as whether you should go to a party or to a team practice. It depends on what kind of experience you want and how successful you want to be at your chosen activity. In high school, I always chose hockey over a party. I knew other parties would come up—ones that would fit into my schedule. I wanted the experiences of being an elite athlete and being good in school. My friends who were really my friends always understood and supported me. Many of my friends from my younger days are still my great friends today, even though I missed out on a lot of social activities.

> *I looked like a monster. Tears ran down my face. I was so obviously devastated.*

Every experience has a message, and it's not always easy to see the message right away. Following the 2005 World Championship in Sweden—where we lost for the first time in a gold medal game at the World Championship—a picture of me appeared in the Canadian newspapers. I looked like a monster. Tears ran down my face. I was so obviously devastated. When we landed in Canada and I stepped off the plane, there was someone there with a newspaper, and they shoved it in my face. I was so upset. I wanted to phone the newspapers to yell at them for printing such a horrible picture of me.

I'm in the back row, middle, with my team in the Mississauga Girls Hockey League.

Everyone mobs goalie Kim St. Pierre after winning our first Olympic gold in Salt Lake in 2002 after surviving so many short-handed situations.

One of the most enjoyable aspects of being on Team Canada is going to schools to talk about our experiences. Here we visit a school in Antigonish, Nova Scotia.

But I didn't. Instead of berating the newspapers about the horrible photo, I cut it out. From 2005 to 2006, it was a reminder of the disappointment that I had felt with that loss. I didn't want to feel like that after a championship game again. I wanted to see myself smiling, with a gold medal around my neck. Instead of crumpling up the paper and throwing it in the garbage, I used it as a motivational tool. I think that loss from 2005 gave the team the lessons we needed to win in 2006. As a group, we needed that loss to know what it was like to lose. In life, try to use your challenging experiences to make things better.

That loss in Sweden told us that we couldn't take any team for granted. In 2006 in Turin, we faced Sweden in the gold medal game. This was a surprise because Sweden had beaten the U.S.A. to get to the gold medal game. We knew the media and all of Canada expected us to win. In the dressing room, we watched the U.S.A. play Finland for the bronze medal. Seeing the U.S.A. play in that game forced us to reflect. If they could lose as they did in the semi-final, we could potentially lose, too. We knew we couldn't take anything for granted. We knew we had to step on the ice and play as hard as we could. We had learned from experience that no team could be taken lightly.

> *Instead of crumpling up the paper and throwing it in the garbage, I used it as a motivational tool.*

Our victory against Sweden that day was rewarding.

Learning from experience also means learning from those who have travelled the road before you. I learned so much from players like Angela James, France St. Louis, and Stacy Wilson.

I also consider education to be vitally important. Going to school is another great experience. Many of the women on Canada's national teams and Olympic teams have gone on to receive post-secondary educations. We've had girls on our team with degrees from Harvard and Stanford in the U.S. and the University of Toronto and other great Canadian universities. In addition to setting your sights on your sport or activity, it is equally as important to focus on education, too. I think it's important, however, to choose the school that is right for you. Education is an experience that you won't want to miss out on. My experience at Guelph University was one of the best experiences of my life—right up there with any of the gold medals. I have lifelong friends whom I went to school with at Guelph. Playing hockey for the Guelph Gryphons still remains one of the highlights of my career.

> *My experience at Guelph University was one of the best experiences of my life—right up there with any of the gold medals.*

Experience is important to success. It is so important to look for any opportunity that will give you experience, and it is also important to reflect on your experiences and learn from them. Every victory and every defeat is an opportunity to learn something. Every day, in everything you do, you can find some sort of learning experience.

I wake up every morning hoping for new and exciting experiences. On Saturday, October 14, 2006, I was given the opportunity to do the colour commentary on *Hockey Night in Canada*. The Toronto Maple Leafs were playing at home against the Calgary Flames—two great Canadian teams. I had flown to Toronto to do in-between period interviews, not colour commentating. I was at the arena during the morning skate, watching the Leafs practice, when my producer wanted to chat with me. It was then that he asked that I do the colour job because Harry Neale—the usual host—was snowed in at home. This was seven hours before the show! I knew the game would be broadcast to two million viewers. I also knew that I would be scrutinized by those same two million. I phoned my husband, and he supported my decision to accept the honour. Yes, I felt extreme pressure, and I was unbelievably nervous. However, I got through it by telling myself that I had the chance to prove to all of Canada that female hockey players know the game. I thought about all my teammates, and I didn't want to let them down. There was a lot on my shoulders at the time, but I knew I could do it! On the first power play for the Leafs, I actually called the goal before it happened, and the satisfaction of knowing what I had just done made me smile. After that one play, I felt a sense of belonging. I could have declined the opportunity and experience because of such short notice, or I could have used the excuse that no woman had ever held the job before, or I could have said no, simply from fear. But I didn't. I wanted the experience. I enjoyed the experience. This one experience opened many doors for me and led to incredible opportunities.

I enjoyed the experience. This one experience opened many doors for me and led to incredible opportunities.

Just because I'm retired from hockey doesn't mean that I want to stop having experiences.

I'm still learning each and every day.

Experience is the life lessons given to you on a daily basis.

A = ATTITUDE

"Attitude is a way of being. Attitude means believing in your goals and dreams. Attitude can make or break you."

Cassie Campbell

Attitude means believing in yourself, your goals, and your dreams. You must have the belief and attitude that what you're doing is right, and you can't let other people control your success. In my sport—hockey— every country plays to beat Team Canada.

Prior to the 2002 Olympics, the Canadian national women's hockey team lost to the Americans eight times. Eight times! It would have been easy to get down and tell ourselves that we didn't have a chance to win the gold medal. We could have folded and said we couldn't do it.

So many things seemed to be going wrong that season. Our fans and the media were all over us, suggesting that we weren't good enough. And to add to the challenges, one of our veteran players was cut late in the season and was replaced with a younger player, which angered many teammates and created a divide in our dressing room. It was a pretty stressful time, and I honestly felt that any one of us could have been cut. I told everyone in the dressing room, "If you don't think this could have been you, that's where the problem starts." The negative energy in the dressing room was not good. We couldn't win a gold medal with a dressing room full of players who were constantly grumbling and split on an issue that we, as players, had no control over.

> *You must have the belief and attitude that what you're doing is right, and you can't let other people control your success.*

An important part of being a team is sticking together. We had to recognize that this was a wake-up call for the rest of us and that we had to change our collective attitude if we were to work together. Cherie Piper was the young player brought in to replace one of our veterans. The decision for her to assume the veteran's role had been made by our coaching staff. They had the team's best interests in mind when making the change, and we players had to respect it, forget about it, and move on. This was the beginning of a long Olympic journey with our new team member, who deserved to be there. As captain of the team, it was up to me to ensure our team had the right attitude going into the Olympics.

In our eighth and final game in our pre-Olympic tour, we played against the U.S.A. in Vancouver. This was just prior to travelling to Salt Lake City. We outshot the Americans, 32–16, but they beat us, 3–2. We scored the first goal in that game. I remember Caroline Ouellette passed to me, I passed to Hayley, and she scored. It was one of those victorious moments where we clicked. I thought we had them. There was no way we could lose. Then the U.S.A. came back and scored. Then Botts (Jennifer Botterill) scored. We were dominating the game and playing hard hockey. We were up, 2–1. When the U.S.A. tied the game, we were still confident that we were going to win. All we had to do was put the puck in the net one more time. The third U.S.A. goal shocked us. How could that have happened? We beat them to the puck almost every time. We convincingly outplayed them, yet they had just scored the winning goal. After that game, I knew, as captain, I had to show that we still believed we were going to win the gold medal at the Olympics.

There was so much pressure on us. We had really needed the momentum of a win before going to the Olympics.

The 2001–2002 season had been the most difficult hockey year of my life. There was so much pressure on us. We had really needed the momentum of a win before going to the Olympics. The rink in Vancouver was packed, and everyone knew the pressure Canada faced. It would have been easy to hang our heads and file back to the dressing room. I knew I had to do something to boost my teammates' spirits and help them stay strong, or our team would continue to struggle.

Jayna Hefford and Jennifer Botterill, two of the most talented scorers Team Canada has ever seen.

Here I am in my red road Team Canada sweater during the World Championships.

After we patted our goalie on the head, I gathered everyone around the bench and said, "When you shake hands, send a message to every player with your eyes. We have to demonstrate that the loss did not deflate our confidence and that we still have a positive attitude."

We deserved to win that game, even though we didn't. Each player held her head high while shaking hands. I knew they were having a hard time believing we were still going to win. Outside, there was so much negative talk circulating. The fans could see only the score, the loss. They were all over us. They weren't rooting for us.

That night, I witnessed a shift in attitude. In that dressing room, as leaders, Hayley, Vicky, and I said, "Let's talk about the eight in a row. Let's discuss instead of criticize. And let's feel free to show some emotion. There's nothing wrong with showing emotion."

This led to a heart-to-heart discussion. Our team spent over an hour in the dressing room talking and gathering our thoughts. Each of us released a lot of pent-up negative energy, knowing that nothing we were to say would go any further than that room. Nothing would be held against us. As a group, we had to move on and get over it. And we had to face the media. I remember turning to my roommate, Cheryl Pounder, later that night, and saying, "When we win, what a story this will be." That was my theme for the rest of the season.

We deserved to win that game, even though we didn't. Each player held her head high while shaking hands.

We'd lost eight to the U.S.A., but we were still confident about winning the gold medal.

We still believed we were going to win.

Nothing was going to stop us.

As the captain for that 2002 Olympic team, I knew we had to maintain the established momentum and energy. Hayley, Vicky, and I realized that we needed to do something following that night in Vancouver to keep the team positive. If we wanted to win, we had to get our team to stick together. For motivation, we decided to host a dinner and invite some special guests to breathe life into the girls. We wanted to prevent negativity.

It was an incredible video that showed just how far women's hockey had come in a short time.

First, we played a video of the first World Women's Championship that was held in Ottawa in 1990. The players wore white pants and pink sweaters! It was an incredible video that showed just how far women's hockey had come in a short time. It was an inspiring video, and it left us wanting to win for those pioneers who blazed the trail for us—Canadian female hockey players who were fortunate enough to be going to the Olympics.

Dawn McGuire, a dominating figure from that 1990 team, spoke, as did her teammate France St. Louis, who connected via conference call. She spoke in her native French, which helped to unite our team. After these great veteran players spoke, we asked that Catriona Le May Doan visit, as she was named Canada's flag-bearer for the 2002 Olympics.

Paralympian Earle Connor came to talk to our team as well. Earle has only one leg, though he has never allowed his disability to interfere with achieving his goals. He holds a world record in sprinting, and I felt it important for our team to see a person with such a positive attitude. I desperately wanted to change the attitude of our team. They were feeling defeated because of our poor pre-Olympic record. Vicky, Hayley, and I paid for this dinner. We wanted to show that regardless of our eight straight losses, we still believed in our team's abilities to win.

Here I'm waiting to get into the action. Wearing the "C" was a highlight of my career and an enormous responsibility which I took as seriously as playing. Coach Karen Hughes is on the left.

Cherie Piper (left) and Jennifer Botterill are two important reasons we won gold in Turin.

One player said to me, "That was the best night of my life."

We struggled through great adversity, though we ultimately maintained our positive attitude. In our semi-final game against Finland in the 2002 Olympics in Salt Lake City, we were down 3–2 going into the third period. We had never been down against Finland. We'd always beaten them.

We continued to work hard for our goal—never losing sight of our dream and what motivated us to be there. In the dressing room between periods, we talked. I remember saying, "I don't know why we have so many challenges this year, but we're capable of overcoming these obstacles." We beat Finland, 7–3, in that semi-final to advance to the gold medal game against the U.S.A.

All the challenges we faced leading up to that final game were nothing compared to what we were about to face.

> We continued to work hard for our goal—never losing sight of our dream and what motivated us to be there.

The officiating in the gold medal game was terrible. We played an enormous part of the game short-handed. It didn't look good for us. Our team was so focused on winning that gold medal that even though we were up 3–1 after two periods, there was still a sense that we had to play hard in the third period in order to win. There was a lot of emotion in our dressing room between the second and third periods, but then Dana Antal, the quietest person on our team, stood up and spoke. Everyone was so shocked that we all immediately calmed down, listened, and refocused.

We held on, each of us remaining positive. Some of our best players—Danielle Goyette, Jennifer Botterill, Caroline Ouellette, and Dana—didn't get much ice time, as we were handed one penalty after another, which meant our penalty killers played most of the game. Instead of complaining about their lack of play time, they slid down the bench to let the penalty-kill players do their job. Without this level of attitude, we might not have won. They cheered us on and stayed positive. They could have slumped on the bench, but they didn't. They kept a positive attitude for the entire team.

Our 2002 team faced adversity right up until the very last minute. We won Olympic gold by beating the U.S.A., 3–2. The winning goal was scored by Jayna Hefford, with just one second left in the second period. She's an amazing player—one of the best goal scorers in the world.

> *Our 2002 team faced adversity right up until the very last minute. We won Olympic gold by beating the U.S.A., 3–2.*

We all have the option to choose how to live each day: with either a positive or a negative attitude. The attitude that you choose often finds you, so if you go through life with a negative attitude, negative things will come to you. If you go through life with a positive attitude, positive things will come to you. It is important, however, to ensure that a positive attitude is held with modesty. You can think you're good—that's okay—but there's a difference between being cocky and being humble.

Over the years, I've had a few favourite slogans that have to do with attitude. Our team had a slogan in 2006: "Take care of yourself. Take care of each other." Though it was important to take my own game to new levels, it was also important to understand the team's philosophy and goals. None of the players or staff members ever put themselves before the team. They all had great attitudes.

Many female hockey players have great attitudes. Growing up, most of us were told, "Girls shouldn't play hockey." Had any of us listened to those negative comments, we wouldn't have experienced the opportunities that hockey provided.

H.E.A.R.T.

Goalie Kim St. Pierre has been in net for so many big games for Canada, and deservedly so.
Even in practice we have a tough time scoring on her.

A = Attitude **47**

Gillian Apps (left) and Gillian Ferrari pose with Becky Kellar's son, Owen.

Believing in the goals you set for yourself, as long as they are healthy, is part of having a great attitude.

Someone with a great attitude who impressed me over the years was Dana Antal. She is a great example of what I've been talking about. She had completely blown out her knee, and after considerable rehabilitation, she returned only to break her leg a year later. In between each injury, she made the Olympic team in 2002 and was on the World Championship team in 2004. She continued to push and train. She never complained in front of the team. Not once, but twice, was she injured, and on both occasions she made the team. She was such an inspiration to me.

The oldest player on our 2006 team was Danielle Goyette, and the media focused greatly on her age. Rather than allowing this to affect her attitude, she trained and worked hard and never used her advanced years as an excuse or crutch. Instead, it motivated her. In Italy, our youngest player was Meghan Agosta. Instead of being jealous of her age and young legs, Danielle relied on humour and was often heard saying, "I'm old enough to be your mother." Danielle Goyette's attitude and work ethic allowed her to be Canada's flag-bearer in those 2006 Olympics. There are few people capable of competing at an Olympic level at the age of 41.

Not once, but twice, was she injured, and on both occasions, she made the team. She was such an inspiration to me.

Kim St. Pierre, our starting goalie in 2002, was a huge part of our gold medal success, though in 2006, she was named our number-two goalie. She accepted this decision and came to the team meeting the following morning with an incredibly positive attitude. She never let her personal disappointment bother our starting goalie, Charline Labonté. She could have come to our meeting bitter, but she didn't. That's attitude. In fact, Kim went on the next year to be the starting goalie and won Canada's ninth gold medal at the 2007 World Championship in Winnipeg. That same year, Sami Jo Small was named our third goalie. She was supportive even though the decision was not in her favour. The night before our gold medal game, she gave me a good luck card as encouragement. To me, this was a really touching behind-the-scenes moment, and Sami Jo showed a lot of class and a great attitude.

> *Becky never complained about the lack of time off, and she never used this as an excuse if she had an off night.*

Our team was based in Calgary during our 2006 Olympic preparation. While this western city made sense for many reasons, it wasn't exactly the most convenient for some of our players. Becky Kellar, for example, lived in Toronto, though she moved not only herself to Calgary but also her toddler son, Owen. Our team's hectic schedule required that she hire a nanny so she could train, though her husband, while supportive of the situation, remained in Toronto due to work responsibilities. When we flew to Europe for pre-Olympic competition, she left a day before us to stop in Toronto to drop Owen off with his dad. She then went on to meet us in Europe. When we flew home, tired and exhausted, she flew to Toronto instead of Calgary, and while we enjoyed a day off, her parenting responsibilities meant that she didn't, as picking up her son meant an extra day of travel for her.

Our coach, Melody Davidson, would say, "Becky, take a day off." But she wouldn't. Becky's answer was always, "No, Mel. I want to be treated like everyone else." Becky never complained about the lack of time off, and she never used this as an excuse if she had an off night. Her attitude was amazing, and her ability to balance motherhood and being a professional hockey player was remarkable. She recognized her responsibilities and, for that, earned tremendous respect from her entire team.

Our team is made up of both English- and French-speaking players. The team's official language, however, is English, which proved challenging for our French-speaking players—particularly when listening to coaching instructions in their second language. They all demonstrated amazing attitude, however, and adapted. They were truly amazing, and the experience of playing on Team Canada resulted in all the French players becoming bilingual.

> *They were truly amazing, and the experience of playing on Team Canada resulted in all the French players becoming bilingual.*

At the 2006 Olympics, our coach, Melody Davidson, created coins that displayed each player's name on one side and our team slogan on the other. The idea was to solidify us as a team, and Melody explained that each player would draw a coin from a bag and then speak about the player on that coin. Our fitness trainer, Jason Poole, got my name. He talked about how humble I was and that he was surprised that I didn't have a big attitude because I was captain of the best women's hockey team in the world. His words meant the world to me because attitude is so important to me. I truly believe that a good attitude can lead you to success.

Attitude means believing in yourself and your goals and being humble in your successes. It can make or break you. Always live life with a positive attitude, even when times are tough.

CHAPTER FOUR

R = RESPONSIBILITY AND RESPECT

"Responsibility and respect are not just things you think about but things you do."

Cassie Campbell

Becoming an adult brings with it a lot of responsibilities. But kids have a lot of responsibilities, too. Kids are responsible for helping around the house and chipping in with family roles. Being involved in sports can teach so much about responsibility and how to manage time. Through playing hockey and other sports in my younger years, I learned a lot about responsibility. My parents divorced when I was young, leaving my mom single. I knew that my mom needed help and that I would have to offer my support. I did a lot of jobs around the house and had to complete my chores before I was allowed to play hockey. I had to make sure the house was clean, and I tell you, I had more than just one chore. I had many.

I started my first job at the age of 14. I was a waitress at a restaurant that catered primarily to kids, and I would work ten or so hours a week, serving birthday parties. The restaurant had a mouse mascot costume, and one day, I was required to be the mouse. Rowdy customers would often pull at my costume and attempt to topple me over. My paycheque, however, compensated for the aggravation and provided me with some spending money. Now, I'm not saying that all kids should go out and get a job at 14. In fact, my father didn't want me to be employed at such a young age, and he probably doesn't know I worked at a restaurant—until now. At that age, however, I felt the responsibility to pay for the fun things that I liked to do. My mother always said my first responsibility was school and my second responsibility was helping around the house. Only then was I allowed to maintain an active interest in a sport or hobby. (I had to have those three things in order before I could take on the job). I chose hockey to keep me active, among many other sports and clubs. I think that staying active and keeping up with schoolwork and working a minimal few hours a week helped

> *The restaurant had a mouse mascot costume, and one day I was required to be the mouse.*

me to become a successful athlete. I learned how to manage my time and get the most from every hour of the day. I learned how to be responsible for myself, my team, and my family, and I learned how to have balance in my life.

Not all kids can go out and get a job, but you can show some responsibility today by just taking care of your own equipment. If you're too small to carry your heavy bag, then carry your stick. And all of you can air out your equipment when you get home. Don't leave these jobs to your mom or dad because they're not the ones playing the sport. When you get older and stronger, then it's your responsibility to carry your own equipment bag. You can also make sure your bag is packed properly and that you have everything you need to play when you get to the arena. It's also important to understand and know that your equipment is expensive and that, likely, someone has spent money to ensure that you have it. You have a responsibility to make it last as long as possible. These may seem like little things, but they are stepping stones to learning about responsibility.

> *If you're too small to carry your heavy bag, then carry your stick.*

It is so important to take responsibility for all of your actions—both big and small. For the Salt Lake City games, our team came up with a slogan. Our slogan was W.A.R., which stood for *We Are Responsible.* This slogan came from our loss at the 1998 Nagano games. We were each to be responsible for our actions, both on and off the ice, so we were not going to have any excuses in 2002. In order to be successful, we had to stop pointing fingers. As a group, this was important, and it allowed us to collectively accept responsibility as a team. It's far easier to point blame at others. No matter what, always take responsibility for your own actions.

I started my career as a forward and later moved back to defence. Both require different responsibilities, and both are fun to play at the highest level.

Each year we get a themed T-shirt. For the 2006 Olympics our slogan was
"Take care of yourself; take care of one another.

Some of you may go on to become team leaders. If you get lucky enough to wear the "C" on your sweater, it is your responsibility to know what makes your teammates tick and to understand each and every personality. You have to learn how and when to motivate people. I was tremendously lucky to wear the "C" for many years, exactly 50 international games. As captain, I felt I had more than just my on-ice responsibilities. I had a responsibility to the dressing room, to each individual teammate, and to my country.

There are many ways to motivate others. In 1997, aboard the bus to play against the U.S.A. in a game in Kitchener, Ontario, I made everyone a necklace. At the time, both teams were equally matched, so the games were always close. In my younger years, I wasn't much of a napper, so I took the time while others slept to make these crazy necklaces with a bunch of stuff I had purchased. They were made of red ribbons and had gold hearts on them. On the bus, I made a speech about how we had to work as a team and play with heart, and then I handed out the gifts. We beat the U.S.A. in overtime, and I was delighted to learn that all the girls wore their necklaces during the game. At the time, I felt it my responsibility to unite the team and bring everyone together. I wanted to make the girls understand that to win, we had to play as a team. Everyone had to know that we weren't going to win on individual skills alone.

> *I had a responsibility to the dressing room, to each individual teammate, and to my country.*

Hopefully, some of you may go on to become a member of Canada's national team, or to reach the pinnacle of your chosen field. Anyone who has ever played on a national team knows that to be responsible, you have to give back to the game and take it to the next level. As women hockey players, we're constantly trying to improve. We train hard and pave the road for those players to follow.

Geraldine Heaney contributed to Canada's hockey program for many years. She was a great player and an example of someone who gave back to the game. She retired after the 2002 Olympics. I looked up to her as a strong defenceman. She played at the first World Women's Championship in 1990 and scored an amazing goal that made TSN's top ten goals for the year. This included all the goals from the men in the NHL! Now she's coaching women's hockey in the CIS (Canadian Intercollegiate School) system and teaching young women her passion for the game. A lot of my teammates have started hockey schools to help young girls become better hockey players.

> *Although we were tired, we knew it was important to carry on and create traditions for our sport.*

In 2005, while we were playing in Regina, our coach put Vicky and I in charge of a team-building exercise that revolved around the history of women's hockey. Though we were exhausted and the last thing we wanted to do was play a game, we knew we had to do this because our coach had asked us to. We created a trivia game that tested our knowledge of the game. It brought the group together in an enjoyable atmosphere of fun and encouragement. Although we were tired, we knew it was important to carry on and create traditions for our sport. The young players asked so many questions about the first World Championship team of 1990 and every team that followed. A lot of the jokes from that night kept us going for the entire year. Now that I'm retired, I'm thrilled that some of those young players will become veterans and remember the values we instilled. It will be their responsibility to carry on the traditions we started as well as to create new ones.

We often visited schools when travelling across Canada as part of the national team. We even visited some schools when travelling through Sweden. As players, we understood

*The fan support we have received across the country is phenomenal
as this long lineup for autographs attests.*

I'm hamming it up with a plastic statue of Ronald McDonald in the Olympic village cafeteria. I started working for McDonald's in 1997 and in 2003 started a street hockey tournament in support of Ronald McDonald House of Southern Alberta. Many Olympic athletes from different countries have put their autographs on this Ronald.

how important it is to sign autographs and attend public events. Many of us have donated our time by speaking at kids' banquets or attending other events, such as Esso Fun Days, introductory clinics to women's hockey, or Chevrolet Safe and Fun hockey clinics and seminars. We wanted to do this to give back and to help the sport. It was our responsibility to share our hockey success with other people.

I started a street hockey tournament in Calgary in 2003, and all the proceeds from the tournament go toward the Ronald McDonald House of Southern Alberta. The Ronald McDonald House is a safe, fun place for children who are undergoing life-saving treatments at nearby children's hospitals. It is a home away from home for these children and their families. I really wanted to help start something that would be a legacy. I wanted to raise money for a good cause and give back to the community; after all, I had won a gold medal. I felt it was my responsibility to share this medal with the people in my country who supported me. I definitely owed something to Canada and Canadians. I have also helped out with World Vision, an organization that helps children in other countries who are less fortunate than us. In fact, I went to El Salvador to meet the young girl who my parents sponsored for eleven years. She is flourishing because of my parents' generous donations over the years.

> *I felt it was my responsibility to share this medal with the people in my country who supported me.*

When you're put on a pedestal by your country, I think it's important to give back and share success with supporters, young children in particular. I enjoy working with children and offering inspiration. I guess that's why I wanted to write this book—to share so much with you. At the same time, I don't think you have to be famous or an adult to give back. Being a volunteer is one of the greatest experiences you can have. With my annual street hockey tournament, I feel that if I can have an impact and put a smile on the face of a child who has cancer, or is battling another life-threatening challenge, then I want to do that.

Responsibility and respect go together because respect is action-driven. You can't just think respect; you have to practice it. And you have to respect yourself first and foremost. You have to respect your goals and dreams as long as they are healthy and happy ones. When I was growing up, many people advised me against being a hockey player. Regardless of outside influence, I decided that I wanted to be one anyway. I respected myself and my game, and I wanted to play. No one was going to bring me down and tell me I couldn't be a hockey player. I didn't allow the opinions of others to alter my dreams. I had respect for my dreams, even when others didn't.

> *You can't just think respect; you have to practice it. And you have to respect yourself first and foremost.*

If you respect yourself, it is a lot easier to respect those around you. People also respect others that take pride in themselves. Though we may differ, we have to respect each other and our differences.

I learned the respect lesson the hard way. When I was playing bantam hockey, a girl speared me, for which she was penalized. On her way to the penalty box, I retaliated and cross-checked her from behind. I got kicked out of the game. I got undressed and then went to the lobby, where my mom was waiting for me.

She said, "Drop your bag and give me your skates."

Confused, I unzipped my bag and then handed her my skates. For the first few minutes of the car ride, she didn't say anything to me. I knew enough to be quiet. You don't mess with my mom!

My individual portrait from 1983-84 when I played with the Brampton Canadettes!

Me and Meghan Agosta, the young rookie sensation who scored a hat trick on her 19th birthday against Russia in her first of many Olympics.

We were almost halfway home when she spoke again, words that, to this day, I'll never forget.

She said, "I don't ever want to see you treat someone like that again. Never. Not anyone. During a game or not. You treat people with respect, no matter what they do to you. What you did was totally unnecessary and dirty. If you ever do that again, you will never play hockey again."

I had to do a lot of grass cutting, laundry, and dishes to get my skates back. And I had to phone my coach to tell him I wouldn't be at hockey until my mom returned my skates. I tell you, that was a long two weeks for me. But I learned my lesson. I really respected my mother for being so hard on me and showing me that what I had done was wrong.

A lot of young players wear the red "Respect" or "STOP" sign on the back of their jerseys. Personally, I think the development and creation of these patches was a great idea. Players wear them with the hope that they will make others around them think before they act. Hockey organizers have placed the warning stop signs on the back of players' jerseys with the intent that they will reduce hitting from behind. Serious injuries can result when a player hits another player from behind. This type of action is completely unsportsmanlike and shows no respect for one's opponent. Those little red patches on the backs of minor hockey jerseys are great reminders to all of us to respect our opponents and everyone at the rink. It's important to respect yourself, your parents, your friends, your teammates, and your opposition, too.

> *Responsibility and respect are not just things you think about, but things you do.*

All people in this world are responsible for their own actions, and all people in this world must respect themselves so they can, in turn, respect others.

Responsibility and respect are not just things you think about, but things you do.

T = TEAMWORK

"When everyone is willing to work together to do the little things that can make a big difference, you have a great team."

Cassie Campbell

Teamwork is important to the success of any team. I've always found that team-building activities offer teams the opportunity to work together outside of the hockey arena. Team-building is essential because you get to know each other, and the more you know about each other, the more you trust, and the more you trust, the more you're willing to fulfill your own role on the team. You don't have to be the best of friends with everyone, but you do have to work together.

For me, when it came to playing, I wanted to be able to look down the bench and know that I could trust everyone I played with. I didn't hang out outside of hockey with everyone I played with, but when it came to the team, I knew we had to work together. Sometimes team-building might seem tedious, but something good always comes out of it. Team-building also creates long-lasting memories. We often did fun things outside of hockey, like curling, playing cards, or going to the movies. Such events gave us quality time with one another.

We often did fun things outside of hockey, like curling, playing cards, or going to the movies.

Prior to the 2002 Olympics, we spent some time in a place called Emerald Lake, just outside of Banff, Alberta. We did mazes and puzzles and other team-building exercises. Everyone had to work together in order to figure out the puzzle games. One game required us to figure out how to retrieve a glass from within a roped-off circle without stepping or reaching inside the circle with our hands. All we had to help us was an elastic band and some string. And we had to do this within a time limit. I tell you, this sort of game, with such strict rules, gave everyone an opportunity to see who listened and who didn't. It also allowed each group to access individual strengths. Sami Jo, our goalie at the time, had an engineering degree from Stanford, so we decided to rely on her knowledge while we worked together on this task. She helped us figure out how to get the elastic around the glass, and then we each took turns pulling, to draw the glass closer to the edge of the rope. This exercise taught us how to work as a team and use individual strengths to complete a task.

> My stomach got queasy just watching them swinging as the entire apparatus shook. And we had to do this next!

My experience on the national team showed me that sometimes team-building exercises are made crazy hard in order to get people out of their comfort zones. During an exercise in Valcartier, Québec, at a Canadian army training centre, we were asked to come to a field with long pants and T-shirts on. The day was scorching hot, and when we arrived, we watched 20 Canadian soldiers preparing for their peacekeeping mission in Bosnia. They were wearing more than 100 pounds of gear and were made to run an obstacle course. One of the obstacles had rope ladders that hung from a shaky contraption that looked like an oversized soccer goal with two tall posts and a long crossbar. The object of the course was to climb up the swinging rope ladders and get over the crossbar, which was set at a height taller than some houses. I thought this course looked really dangerous. I held my breath watching the soldiers climb the rope ladder to get up and over the crossbar. My stomach got queasy just watching them swinging as the entire apparatus shook. And we had to do this next!

Once the soldiers manoeuvred the rope ladders, there was another obstacle with barbed wire. They had to crawl underneath it, trying not to get snagged. They also went over cement walls and climbed up ropes. It took the soldiers at least an hour to get through the course.

Then our coach, Danièle Sauvageau, said, "Girls, it's your turn."

Playing and practicing on ice are fun but it's important to get into the gym regularly to work on the basics of body fitness as well.

The entire team poses in front of an enormous Canadian flag in Turin during the 2006 Olympics. We're all wearing our official gear from the opening ceremonies.

We thought she was absolutely crazy. The soldiers had struggled and were completely exhausted when they finished, so how did she expect us to do the same thing? We were hockey players. Interestingly enough, some girls chose not to do this. Those of us who did were scared, knowing it was dangerous, but we were up for the challenge. We were split into two teams. At first, it was a mad race to see who could get through the fastest, as the first reaction was to get it over with as quickly as possible. Instant competitiveness! The reality of the situation was that we couldn't get through this obstacle course as individuals; we weren't trained soldiers, so we had to get through it as a team. We had to step back and say, "We have to do this together to make it work." I was a good climber, so I offered to climb the cement wall first. I told everyone that I could get over and then catch them as they descended on the other side. I fell when I went over, but fortunately, I landed on sand. By going over first, I was able to help those who were not as skilled at climbing. By the end of it, we had blisters and bruises but were happy to have made it through. This team-building exercise got us out of our comfort zones. Each individual had to challenge themselves to the extreme for the good of the team.

By the end of it, we had blisters and bruises but were happy to have made it through.

Now, not all team-building exercises produce that much pain. In fact, some are really fun, particularly our team meals. During our 2005 training camp in Prince Edward Island, we each lived in cottages. Monday and Wednesday nights were meal nights, where one cottage had to cook for another. We continually switched it around so that each cottage spent one night cooking and one night enjoying a break as another cottage prepared the meal. This gave everyone a chance to get to know everyone, too. The funny thing was that these meal nights became very competitive. Being elite athletes, we each tried to outdo each other. This competitive spirit made everyone in the cottage work together because we were forced to hang out to prepare a meal. In the end, it became so much fun that two cabins would work together to cook for two other cabins.

I realize that not all players will experience the team-building exercises that I've been fortunate enough to take part in with Hockey Canada. But there are things that all players can do. One really simple way to build team spirit is through warm-up exercises. We played foot hockey before every game in 2002 at Salt Lake City. We played East versus West, so all the girls from Ontario and farther east were on one team, and all the girls from west of Ontario played for the other. No matter what rink we were at, we had to find a space to play foot hockey. Looking for a place was a team effort in itself, and collectively, we arranged a makeshift area for play—sometimes moving garbage cans or boxes or whatever to make the space for our game. Some players were refs, and we made it a team affair. I remember we all got a good laugh when the ball bounced off my shin and into the goal, causing my East team to lose the "foot hockey championship."

> *Quickly, we had to overcome this loss, and in one week, we had regrouped and come together as a new team.*

The exercises I've described are all controllable situations that help to build a team, but sometimes teams have to come together due to situations beyond their control. In 2001, Hayley Wickenheiser hurt her knee at the Esso Nationals and couldn't play the World Championship that year. She was one of our best players, so losing her was a tremendous blow to our team. Quickly, we had to overcome this loss, and in one week, we had regrouped and come together as a new team. The many players who previously complained about a lack of ice time now stepped up to fill the void. When you're given this kind of opportunity, it's important to make it work. We won that championship without one of our best players. Jennifer Botterill was always our second-line centre to Hayley. Jennifer recognized the incredible opportunity to showcase her talent as well as the incredible responsibility to support her team, so she contributed 100 percent on that first line, and as a result, won the Most Valuable Player award for that tournament.

Other team-building efforts are created especially for specific groups. In January 2006, during a conversation with another player just before the Turin Olympics, I noted a lack of appreciation for our defensive players. None of them really played on the power play, and they weren't in the glory roles. Our leadership group wanted to do something to demonstrate that we appreciated them, so we created the "Day of the Defenceman." We had Hockey Canada T-shirts made for each defensive player. On the left front was a personal inscription, unique to that individual player, and on the right was the word "Rock," as we felt that our defence was our foundation—the rock of the team. On one sleeve was a picture of a house, symbolizing their role as the protectors of our home—our net. And on the other sleeve was the slogan "Country Roads," which was the defence's favourite song (they often sang this song loudly in the dressing room before games). It was their theme song. The back of each shirt showed each player's number and nickname. With the help of Hockey Canada, we also created a ten-minute video tribute to the defence, to let them know how much we appreciated them. One by one, they each came up to get their T-shirts. Hayley, Vicky, and I stood at the front and handed them out. The defence were so excited, and they put the shirts on right away. Most of them said that it was the best shirt that they ever received, noting that they had never had anything so personalized. We even made one for Caroline Ouellette because she played both forward and

On one sleeve was a picture of a house, symbolizing their role as the protectors of our home—our net.

defence. This gesture helped demonstrate to the entire team the importance of our defence. As forwards, we needed the defence to move the puck up to us so that we could get to the net and score. Every position on a team is important, and every position contributes to the win. Those T-shirts bonded our team, and I think this contributed to our gold medal victory, although I always knew our defence would play as well as it did.

To me, teamwork starts at the top. I've been lucky to have had a lot of good coaches over the years: Sue Scherer, Danièle Sauvageau, Ken Dufton, Rick Osborne, and of course, my mom, who coached me through minor hockey. But the coaching staff that worked best and completely as a team was the group of 2006. The teamwork that our coaching staff displayed before the Turin Olympics was tremendous. Melody Davidson, Tim Bothwell, Margot Page—they all understood their roles and had fun working together, which flowed down to the players. In order for us to be successful, the leadership and direction had to start at the top. A lot of the team-building ideas I have shared with you came from this group of coaches.

But the coaching staff that worked best and completely as a team was the group of 2006.

Once in a while, a player with amazing team spirit makes the national team. When Caroline Ouellette came to our team, she was young and quiet. For me to have been able to see her grow over the years and become such a team player and leader was a wonderful experience. Now, she confidently shows and speaks of her passion and commitment. In 2006, she was frustrated to have to play both forward and defence, but she handled that role very well for our team. She interacted with all the players. She was a forward and a defence, and accepted that role for the good of the team. In a way, she became a bridge that linked us

Here I am with our phenomenal coach, Melody Davidson, who took us to Olympic gold in 2006. Although she demanded a lot from her athletes, she was always fair and honest.

*Prior to every international game we crowded around the goal to say
a few last-minute things and start the game off together.*

We're getting ready to sing O Canada after winning the gold medal in Turin.

all together. She's a great example of a team player, and I have been impressed with her development as a team leader.

Sometimes teamwork goes way beyond your own team. When I was chosen to go to the Olympics, I trained as part of the Canadian national women's hockey team, but when I arrived at the games, I became a member of a greater team—Team Canada—with all the other athletes who were representing our country in their various sports.

I love Catriona Le May Doan and respect her greatly. She is an inspirational athlete, and I felt that having her speak to our team prior to the 2002 Olympics in Salt Lake City was a huge motivator. She graciously accepted my invitation and spoke to our team in both official languages, which further created unity among our players. Her presence was a thrill for each player and made us truly feel part of our nation's team. After her ten-minute speech, I got up and gave her a gift, thinking she would have to go. Although she had an incredibly busy schedule, she stayed to field questions from the players. This was a team-building event, and as flag-bearer, Catriona understood her role as a captain of the bigger team called Canada and knew that she had a responsibility to athletes from each sport.

> **Although she had an incredibly busy schedule, she stayed to field questions from the players.**

That same Olympics, we created a psych-up game. Each player was in charge of a psych-up day and had the responsibility to motivate and possibly make everyone laugh. On the gold medal game day, Vicky Sunohara, Danielle Goyette, and I were in charge. We went to Jamie Salé and David Pelletier, who at the time were Canada's top figure skaters, and asked them to come to talk to our team. We weren't sure if they had the time to speak to us, but we thought we would try anyway. During this Olympic Games, Jamie and David had received an incredible amount of media attention. They skated a flawless performance but had received only the silver medal. The world was outraged with the judging. Everyone who had watched their performance knew they deserved to win. Their faces were on the front of every major newspaper worldwide, and their controversial story earned them interest from all major media, including an invitation to appear on *The Tonight Show* with Jay Leno. This spotlight, however, did not change them. They took the time to come down to our meeting at 8:00 a.m. on the morning of our final game. They didn't have to do this, but they did. This showed me that they were great team players. They didn't see themselves as celebrities. They were figure skaters, and a part of 200 athletes who represented Canada.

> They took the time to come down to our meeting at 8:00 a.m. on the morning of our final game.

They told us they were going to be at our final game and that they thought it was important to come to talk to us. I was blown away and so happy when, after an appeal, they were actually awarded the gold medal for their perfect performance.

It is amazing what a group of people can do together to make great things happen. Our Canadian women's hockey program has been so successful because a group of great individuals—not just one or two—have worked hard to take the game to new levels. I have been so fortunate to play alongside some of the greatest ambassadors of women's hockey.

Teamwork is about doing the little things that can make a big difference. To have a successful team, everyone has to be willing to work together. Little things add up to big things, and everyone on a team has a role to play.

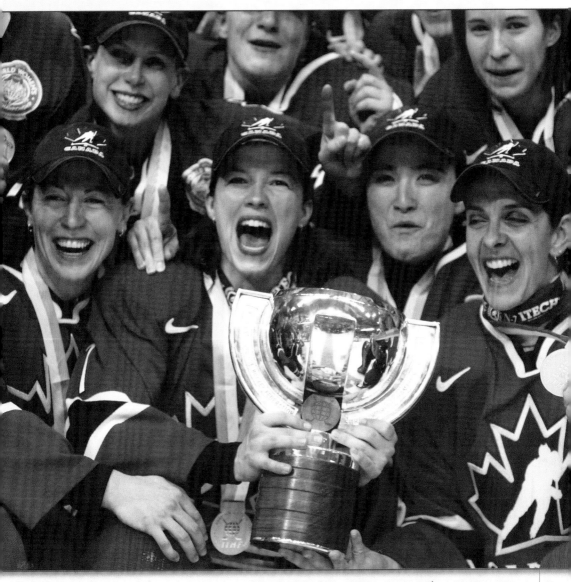

The best feeling in the world, posing for the team portrait on ice after winning the World Championship in Halifax in 2004!

CASSIE'S CONCLUSION

I am sure that after reading this book, you can now understand why I had so much fun playing hockey. Years from now, I may not remember the exact events that lead to all the medals, but I will remember the many people I met along the way.

My hockey career has given me so much to be thankful for, but the most important thing is that it taught me how to push myself every day to become a better player and better person. Hockey taught me to give back to those around me and to believe in my dreams, even when people told me my dreams were impossible.

Because of hockey, I have balance in my life—something that is essential for every person. My sport showed me the importance of being active while also getting a great education. It taught me to understand that, although times may get tough, having a great attitude toward life will go a long way. Hockey helped me to respect myself and be strong in my positive choices. It helped me to learn through different circumstances about leadership and friendship. My international and club experiences in hockey taught me what hard work is and that, in order to succeed, you need to learn to work with many different types of people.

I hope you enjoyed reading *H.E.A.R.T.* My goal was for you to take things from this book that will help you to live your life to the fullest. It doesn't matter whether you play hockey or not, as I believe the information in this book can help you achieve any goal.

Please note that proceeds from this book will be going to The Ladies First Foundation. This foundation will help all Canadian female hockey players as they train for the 2010 Olympics and beyond.